William F. Sudds

Anthem Gems

Composed, Selected and Arranged for Chorus or Quartette Choirs

William F. Sudds

Anthem Gems
Composed, Selected and Arranged for Chorus or Quartette Choirs

ISBN/EAN: 9783337296711

Printed in Europe, USA, Canada, Australia, Japan

Cover: Foto ©Thomas Meinert / pixelio.de

More available books at **www.hansebooks.com**

ANTHEM GEMS.

VOL. I.

Composed, Selected, and Arranged

—FOR—

CHORUS OR QUARTETTE CHOIRS,

—BY—

W. F. SUDDS.

ᜈᜈNOTICE.ᜈᜈ

To the Organist to whose lot it may fall to play these Anthems on the Reed Organ, and who may possibly be unacquainted with the capacity and construction of the Pipe Organ, the following brief explanations may be found useful :

Passages marked Gt. or Gt. Op. Dia., should be played loud and prominent.

Passages marked Sw. or Swell Org., should be played softly.

Passages marked 8 ft., should be played with stops giving tones of absolute pitch.

Passages marked 4 ft., indicate that a stop sounding an octave above absolute pitch may be added to 8 ft. tones or stops.

ᜈᜈCONTENTS.ᜈᜈ

I WILL EXTOL THEE.

Allegro moderato. **W. F. SUDDS.**

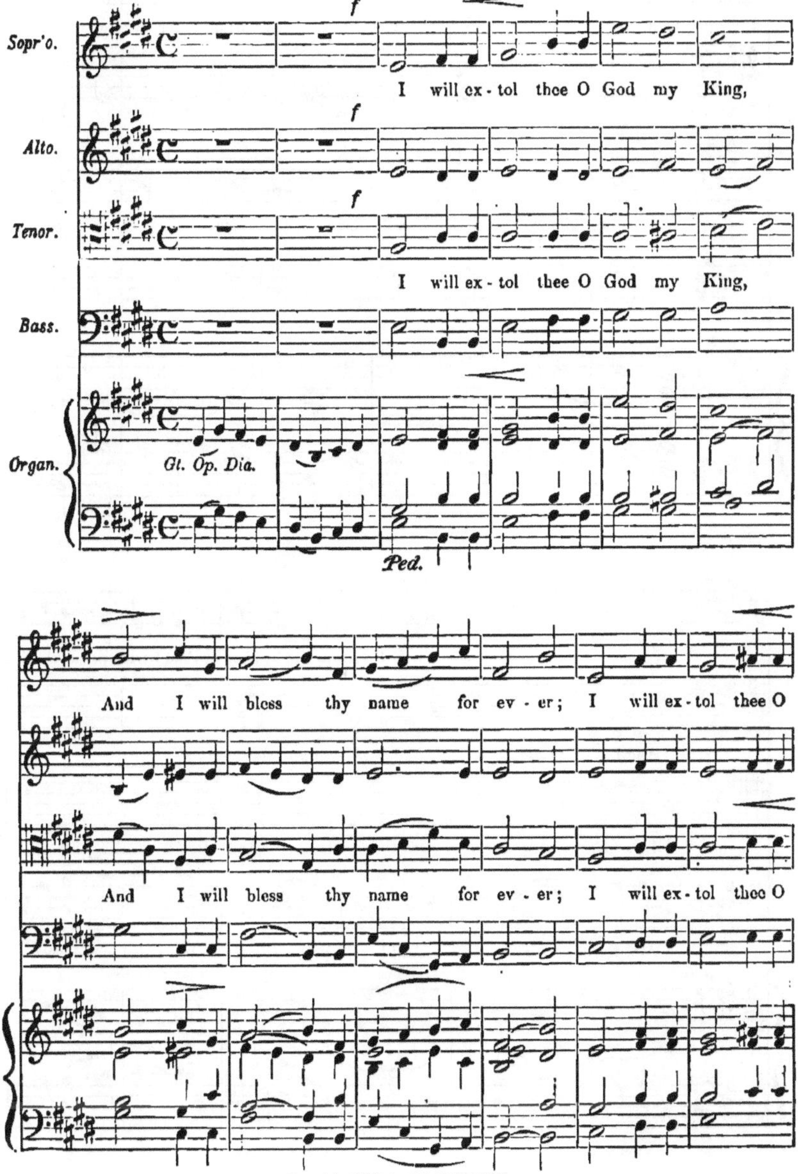

God, my King; And I will bless thy name for ev - er,

And

God, my King; And I will bless thy name for ev - er, and

And I will praise thee, And I will praise thee,

And I will praise thee, And I will praise thee,

I......... .... will praise thee, And I......... .... will

And I will praise thee, And I will praise thee, And I will praise thee

I will extol thee.

And I will praise thee, and I will bless thy name for ev - er,

And I will praise thee, and I will bless thy name for ev - er,

praise thee, and I will bless thy name for ev - er,

And I will praise thee, and I will bless thy name for ev - er, And

And I will praise thee, and I will praise thee, and I will praise thy name for ever-

And I will praise thee, and I will praise thee, and I will praise thy name for ever-

And I will praise thee, and I will praise thee, and I will praise thy name for ever-

I will praise, and I will praise, and I will praise thy name for ever.

I will extol thee

more............ Thou wilt sus - tain me,

ev - er more, Thou wilt sus-

ev - er more,

more............

p Sw. Gt.

Thou wilt sus- tain me, Thou wilt sus - tain me, and com - fort me,

tain, sus - tain - me Thou wilt sus - tain me, and com - fort me,

thou wilt sus- tain me, Thou wilt sus - tain me, and com - fort me,

thou wilt sus - tain me, wilt sus - tain me, and com - fort me,

I will extol thee.

And I will praise thee, and I will praise thee, and I will praise thy name for

And I will praise thee, will praise thee, and I will praise thy name for

And I will praise thee, and I will praise thy name for

And I will praise thy name, will praise thy name for

ev - er more, for ev - er more, for ev - er more.

ev - er more, for ev er more, for ev - er more.

I will extol thee.

"THERE IS A FOUNTAIN."

(HYMN ANTHEM.)

From "CONCONE."

Andante.   1st stanza Solo.   1. There is a fount-ain

Andante.   3d stanza Duet.   3. E'er since, by faith I

p Sw.

filled with blood Drawn from Im - man - uel's veins;   And   sin - ners

saw the stream, Thy flow - ing wounds sup - ply,   Re - deem - ing

plunged be - neath that flood loose all   their guilt - y   stains.

love has   been my theme, And shall   be   till I   die.

2. The dy - - ing thief re - joiced to see That
4. And when this fee - - ble falt'r - ing tongue Lies

fount - ain in his day;......... And there shall I, though
si - lent in the grave;......... Then in a no - bler,

vile as he, Wash all......... my sins a - way.........
sweet - er song. I'll sing thy pow'r to save.........

There is a fountain.

HE SHALL FEED HIS FLOCK.

W. F. SUDDS.

He shall feed His flock, He shall feed His flock,

He shall feed His flock, shall feed His flock like a shepherd,

And gath-er the lambs in His arms.

He shall feed His flock like a shepherd, And gath - er the lambs in His arms, . . . in His arms, And car - ry them in His bo - som.

He shall feed His flock, He shall feed His flock, He shall feed His

He shall feed His flock, He shall feed His flock, He shall feed His

STOP DIA. coup to GT.

He shall Feed His Flock,—2.

Ped.

flock, shall feed His flock like a shepherd, And

flock, shall feed His flock like a shepherd, And

gath-er the lambs in His arms.

gath-er the lambs in His arms.

He shall feed His flock like a shepherd, And gath - er the

He shall feed His flock like a shepherd, And gath - er the

lambs, And gath - er the lambs in His arms.

lambs, And gath - er the lambs in His arms.

LORD OF THE WORLDS ABOVE.

J. KINKEL.

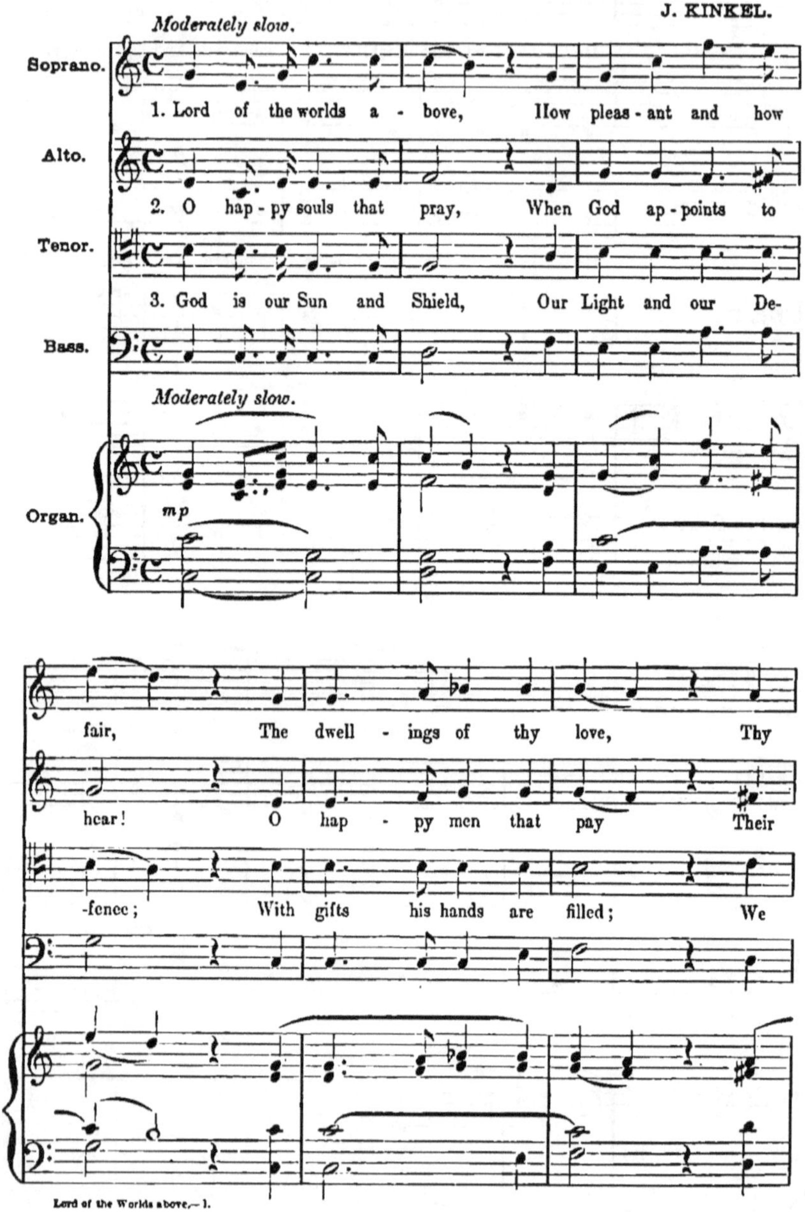

earth - ly tem - ples are! To thine a - bode my heart as-

con - stant ser - vice there! They praise thee still; and hap - py

draw our blessings thence. Thrice hap - py he, O God of

ritard.

-pires, With warm de - sires to see my God.

they That love the way to Zi - - on's hill.

hosts, Whose spir - - it trusts a - lone in thee.

ritard.

BEYOND THE SMILING AND THE WEEPING.

Alto or Bass.

W. F. SUDDS.

1. Beyond the smiling and the weeping, Beyond the waking and the sleeping, Be.
2. Beyond the blooming and the fading, Beyond the shining and the shading, Be.
3. Beyond the parting and the meeting, Beyond the farewell and the greeting, Be.

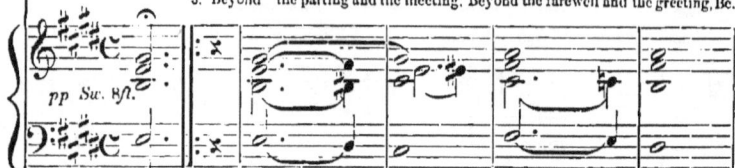

yond the sowing and the reap-ing, I shall be soon, I shall be soon.
yond the hoping and the dreading, I shall be soon, I shall be soon.
yond the pul-se's fer-vor beating, I shall be soon, I shall be soon.

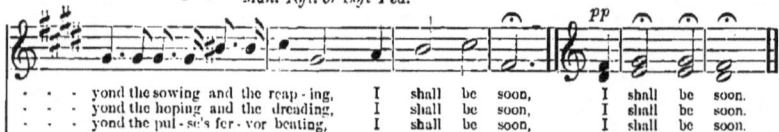

Love, rest and home, Lord tar-ry not,
Sweet, sweet home; But come, but come

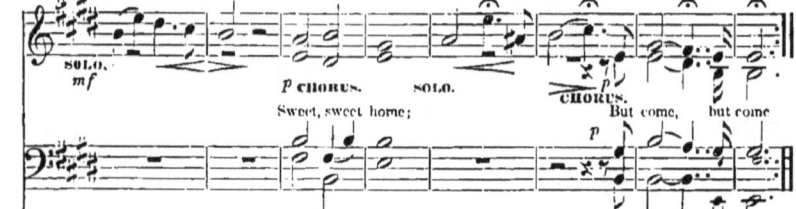

The Organist may repeat last four measures between each two stanzas. Copyright, 1881, by W. F. SHAW.

LIGHT OF THE WORLD.

J. L. HATTON.
Arr. for Choir by W.F. SUDDS.

Moderato.

mf

p

Sop. or Ten.

While I on earth a - bide, Light of the

world . . . . . Be thou my on - ly guide,

Light of the world, Dan - ger alone I

sec.   No hand   out-stretch'd to   me

Save   when   I   turn   to   thee,   Light   of   the   world,

Light   of   the   world.

Soprano.

I   have been lured a · way.   Light   of   the   world

Tenor.

Light of the world

Far from thy paths to stray, Light of the world;
mf
cres.
Like a bark tempest tossed, Rudder and compass lost, 'Til
cres.
Like a bark tempest tossed, Rudder and compass
cres.
dim.
thy beam o'er me crossed, Light of the world.
lost, 'Til thy beam o'er me crossed . . . . .
Rall.
dim.
Light of the world.

Rall.

Quartett or chorus.

Light of the world,

There is an angel band,

Light of the world.

There is an angel band,

Rall.

mf

Light of the world; ... They by thy throne now stand,

Light of the world; ... They by thy throne now stand,

p rall.

Light of the

Light of the

roll.

Light of the world

world. They sing the song of praise, Join in the heavenly lays.

world. They sing the song of praise, Join in the heavenly

world. They sing the song of praise, Join in the heavenly lays.

world. They sing the song of praise, Join in the heavenly

There I my voice would raise, Light of the world, Light of the world.

lays. I my voice would raise, Light of the world, Light of the world.

There I my voice would raise, Light of the world, Light of the world.

lays. I my voice would raise, Light of the world, Light of the world.

Light of the world.

INCLINE THINE EAR TO ME.

HIMMEL.

Swell, 2 Diapasons.

p

Andante.

Dulciana.

mf

8va......................

Solo.—Alto or Bass Voice.

In - cline thine ear, incline thine ear to me, in - cline thine ear, in-

p

dim.

- cline thine ear to me, O Lord, make haste to de - liv - - er me. In-

cres.

dim.

p

- -cline thine ear, in - cline thine ear to me, O Lord, make haste, make haste to de-liv-er me. O save me for thy mercies' sake, O save...... me,

cres.

save me for thy mer-cies' sake. *Great Diapasons.*

mf

QUARTETT.

Sopr'o. Incline thine ear, incline thine ear to me, in-cline thine ear, in-

Alto. Incline thine ear, incline thine ear to me, in-cline thine ear, incline thine

Tenor. Incline thine ear, incline thine ear to me, in-cline thine ear,...... incline

Bass. Incline thine ear, incline thine ear to me, incline thine ear.

Incline thine ear to me.

cline thine ear to me, O Lord, make haste to de - liv - - er me. In-

ear to me, O Lord, make haste to de - liv - - er me. In-

thine ear to me, O Lord, make haste to de - liv - er me.

to me, O Lord, make haste to de - liv - er me. In-

- - cline thine ear, ... incline thine ear to me, O Lord, make haste, make

- cline thine ear, incline thine ear to - me, O Lord, make haste, make

incline thine ear, incline thine ear to me, O Lord, make haste, make haste to de-

- - cline thine ear................ to me,

Incline thine ear to me.

haste to de-liv-er me, O save me for thy mercies' sake, O save........ me,

haste to de-liv-er me, O save me for thy mercies' sake, O save........ me,

..li--ver me, O save me for thy mercies' sake, save, O

O................ Lord,.......................... for thy mercies' sake O

save me for thy mer-cies' sake.

save me for thy mer-cies' sake.

save me for thy mer-cies' sake.

save me for thy mer-cies' sake.

Gt. Diapasons.

mf

Incline thine ear to me.

AND YE SHALL SEEK ME.

SENTENCE.

W. F. SUDDS.

And ye shall seek Me, and find Me,

When ye shall search for Me with all your hearts; Ye shall seek Me, and find Me,

And ye shall seek Me.— 1.

seek Me, and find   Me, When ye shall search for Me with all   your hearts, When ye shall

seek Me, and find   Me, When ye shall search for Me with all   your hearts, When ye shall

search for Me with all   your hearts,   saith   the Lord,   saith   the Lord.

search for Me with all   your hearts,   saith   the Lord,   saith   the Lord.

MARTIN LUTHER'S HYMN.

SOLO and CHORUS.

Great God, what do I see and hear! The end of things cre - a - - - ted; The Judge of man - kind does ap - pear On clouds of glo - ry seat - - ed. The

Martin Luther's Hymn.—4.

trum - pet sounds, the graves re - store The dead which they con-

-tain'd be - fore; Pre - pare, my soul, to meet Him.

CHORUS.
SOPRANO.

Great God, what do I see and hear! The end of

ALTO.

TENOR.

Great God, what do I see and hear! The end of

BASS.

FULL ORGAN.

8ves.
Martin Luther's Hymn.—2.

things cre - a - - ted. The Judge of man - kind does ap-

things cre - a - - ted. The Judge of man - kind does ap-

-pear On clouds of glo - ry seat - - ed. The trum - pet

-pear On clouds of glo - ry seat - - ed. The trum - pet

sounds; the graves re - store The dead which they con-

sounds; the graves re - store The dead which they con-

-tain'd be - fore; Pre- pare, my soul, to meet Him.

-tain'd be - fore; Pre- pare, my soul, to meet Him.

EVENING HYMN.

W. F. SUDDS.

Slowly.

Soprano.
1. The day is past and o - ver; All

Alto.
2. The joys of day are o - ver; I

Tenor.
3. Be Thou my soul's pre - serv - - er, O

Bass.

Slow.

Organ.

thanks, O Lord, to Thee; I pray Thee now that

lift my heart to Thee, And pray Thee that of-

God, for Thou dost know How ma - ny are the'

sin - less The hours of dark may be ; O Je - sus, keep mo

-fence - less The hours of gloom may be ; O Je - sus, make their

per - ils Through which I have to go; O lov - ing Je - sus,

in thy sight, And guard me through the com - ing night.

darkness light, And guard me through the com - ing night.

hear my call, And guard and save me through them all.

Evening Hymn,—2.

Ped.

SOFTLY FADES THE TWILIGHT RAY.

HYMN ANTHEM FOR EVENING SERVICE.

W. F. SUDDS.

1. Soft·ly fades the twi·light ray, Of the ho·ly Sab·bath day, Gently as life's set·ting sun When the christian's course is run; Night her
2. Still the spir·it lin·gers near, When the evening wor·ship·er, Seeks com·munion with the skies, Pressing onward to the prize; Saviour

Sol - emn mantle spreads, o'er the earth as day light fades; All things tell of calm re -
May our sabbaths be days of peace and joy in thee; Till in heav'n our souls re -

Sol - emn mantle spreads, o'er the earth as day-light fades; All things tell of calm re -
May our sabbaths be days of peace and joy in thee; Till in heav'n our souls re -

- - - pose,......... At the ho - ly Sabbath's close.
- - - pose,......... Where the Sabbath ne'er shall close.

- - - pose,......... At the ho - ly Sabbath's close.
- - - pose,......... Where the sabbath ne'er shall close.

Softly fades the twilight ray.

Peace is on the world a broad, 'Tis the hol-y peace of

Peace is on the world a-broad, 'Tis the hol-y peace of

Ped.

God, Sym-bol of the peace with-in, When the spir-it rest from sin.

God,

Sym-bol of the peace with-in, When the spir-it rests from sin.

Rall. *D. S. al Fine.*

Softly fades the twilight ray.

HARK, THE HERALD ANGELS' SING.

From PLEYEL.

1. Hark, hark, hark, the herald angels sing, Glo - ry to the new-born King, Peace on
2. Hail the ho - ly Prince of Peace! Hail the Sun of Righteousness! Light and

(1) earth and mer - cy mild, God and sinners rec - on - ciled, God and
(2) life to all He brings, Joy and healing in His wings, Joy and

sin - ners re - con - ciled, Joy - ful all ye nations rise, Join the

heal - ing in His wings, Let us then with an - gels sing, Glo - ry

tri - umph of the skies; With an - gel - ic host pro - claim, Christ is

to the new-born King! Peace on earth and mer - cy mild, God and

Hark the Herald Angels sing. - 2.

born in Bethle - hem. Hark, hark, hark, the herald angels sing,

sinners rec - on -ciled. Hark, hark, hark, the herald angels sing,

VOICES ALONE.

SW.

Glo - ry, glo - ry, glo - . . - ry to the new-born King.
Glo - ry, glo - ry, glo - ry, glo - ry

Glo - ry, glo - ry, glo- ry, glo - ry, glo - ry to the new-born King.

GT. OP. DIA.

Ped.

Hark. the Herald Angels sing,— 3.

Glory, glo - ry, glo - ry to the new- born King, Glo - ry

Glory, glo - ry, glo - ry to the new- born King, Glo - ry

to the new-born King, Glo - ry to the new-born King, the new-born King.

to the new-born King, Glo - ry to the new-born King, the new-born King.

SWEET THE MOMENTS.

(HYMN ANTHEM.)

W. F. SUDDS.

Sweet the mo-ments rich in bless-ing, Which be-fore the

Life and health and peace pos-sess-ing From the

cross I spend,

Life and health and peace pos-sess-ing From the

sin - ner's dy - ing friend. Tru - ly bless - ed is that sta - tion,

sin - ner's dy - ing friend. Tru - ly bless - ed is that sta - tion,

MAN.

pp SOLI.

Low be - fore the cross to lie, While I see di - vine com-

pp SOLI.

pp SOLI.

Low be - fore the cross to lie, While I see di - vine com-

Ped.

ppp

pas - sion, Beam - ing in his gra - cious eye. Love and grief my

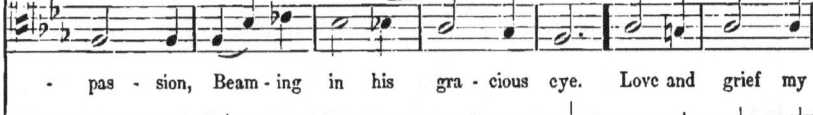

pas - sion, Beam - ing in his gra - cious eye. Love and grief my

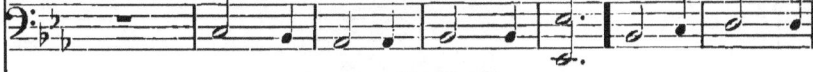

heart di - vid - ing, With my tears his feet I'll bathe; Con - stant

heart di - vid - ing, With my tears his feet I'll bathe; Con - stant

still in faith a - bid - ing Life de - riv - ing from his death.

still in faith a - bid - ing, Life de - riv - ing from his death.

GT. OP. DIA.

1st and 2nd SOP.

,Here in grate - ful, ten - der sor - row, With my Sav-iour will I

SW.

cres. *ppp*

stay. Here new hope and strength I'll bor - row, Here will love my

Here new hope and strength I'll bor - row, Here will love my

GT. OF. DIA.

Ped.

fears a - way, Here will love my fears a - way.

fears a - way, Here will love my fears a - way.

SW. FULL.

Ped.

VESPER HYMN.

Andante Sostenuto.

QUARTETT.

W. F. SUDDS.

1. Soft - ly fades the sun - set splen - dor, And the light of day grows dim; We to thee our prais - es ren - der,

2. Day by day comes rich in bless - ing, Night by night brings ho - calm; Lord to thee our praise ad - dres - ing,

ra'll. dim.   pp

Sing we thus our ves - per hymn. Ju - bi - la - te,

pp

Ju - bi - la - te,

mf

Ri - - ses thus with joy - ful sound. Ju - bi - la te,

rall. dim.

cres.   rall. dim.

Ju - bi - la - - te, Ju - bi - la - te. A - - - men.

Ju - bi - la - - te,

Ju - bi - la - te. A - - - men.

Vesper Hymn.

GOD IS A SPIRIT.

"The Woman of Samaria."
WM. STERNDALE BENNETT.

God is a Spirit.— 1.

worship Him, must worship Him in spirit and in truth.
worship Him, must worship Him in spirit and in truth. God is a
worship Him, ... in spirit and in truth. God is a
wor - ship Him, must worship Him in spirit and in truth.
Ped.
p sw.
cres.
and they that worship Him, must worship Him, must
Spir - it: God is a Spir - it: they must
cres.
Spir - it: God is a Spir - it: worship Him, must
they must
GT.
Ped.

worship *Him* in spir- it and in truth,

wor - ship *Him* in spir- it and in truth, For the Fa - ther seeketh

wor - ship *Him* in spir- it and in truth, For the Fa - ther seeketh

worship *Him* in spir- it and in truth,

MAN.

For the Fa - ther seeketh such, seek - eth such, seek - eth

such, seek - eth such,

such, seek - eth such, seek - eth such, seek - eth

such to worship Him. God is a spir-it, God is a

such to worship Him. God is a spir-it, God is a

spir-it and they that worship Him, and they that worship Him, must

they that worship Him, they that worship Him, must

spir-it, they that worship Him, they, they that worship Him, must

they that worship Him, they that worship Him, must

worship Him, must worship Him, and they that worship Him, and

worship Him, must worship Him, they that worship Him,

worship Him, must worship Him, they that worship Him,

worship Him, they that worship Him,

they that worship Him, must worship Him in spir-it and in

must worship Him, worship Him in spir-it and in

must worship Him, Him in spir-it and in

they that worship Him, Him in spir-it and in

sempre calando.

truth; The Fa - ther seeketh such, For the Fa - ther seeketh

truth; For the Fa - ther seeketh such, For the Fa - ther seeketh

truth; For the Fa - ther seeketh such, seek - eth

sempre calando.

Ped.

such to worship *Him,* to worship *Him,* in spirit and in truth.

such to worship *Him,* to worship *Him,* in spirit and in truth.

sw. *p*

rall.

God is a Spirit.—6.   MAN.   Ped.

SEEK YE THE LORD.
(SENTENCE.)

W. F. SUDDS.

Seek ye the Lord, Seek ye the Lord, Seek ye the Lord,

While he may be found; Seek ye the Lord, Seek ye the Lord,

Call ye up-on him when he is near.

Seek ye the Lord, Seek ye the Lord,

Call ye up-on him, Organ. Call ye up-on him when

he is near, Call ye up-on him when he is near.

O HOW LOVELY IS ZION.

Allegretto non troppo.

From **ROMBERG.**

Sopr'o.

O how lovely, how love-ly is zi-on,

Alto.

Tenor.

O how lovely, how love-ly is zi-on,

Bass.

Accom.

Zi - - on cit - - y of our God, O how

Zi - - on cit - - y of our God, O how

God O how love - - - -

love-ly   is   zi - on, O how love - ly is   zi - - - on

love-ly, how love-ly is   zi - on,

- - - ly, how love-ly is   zi - on, O how love - ly is   zi - - on

cit - y of our God.   O how love - ly,   O how

O how love - ly, how love - - ly

cit - y of our God.

Add 4 ft. Flute.

O how lovely is zion.

love - ly, love - ly is zi - - on cit - y of our God;

O how love - ly is

is zi - - on cit - y of our God;

joy and peace shall dwell in thee, joy............ and

joy and peace shall dwell in thee, joy and

O how lovely is zion.

Soprano Obligato.

peace shall dwell in thee, O how, O how love-ly

Soprano and Alto.

peace shall dwell in thee, O how love-ly, love-ly is

peace shall dwell in thee, O how love ly, love-ly is

cres.

How lovely is zi - on cit - y of our God,

cres.

zi - on, zi - on cit - y of our God; O how

zi - on, zi - on cit - y of our God; O how

cres.

O how lovely is zion.

O how lovely, how lovely is zi - - on cit - - y of our

lovely, love - ly is zi - on, zi - - on cit - y of our

lovely, love - ly is zi - on, cit - y, cit - y of our

cres.

rall. dim.

God; Joy,.......................... joy and peace shall dwell in thee.

f

God; Joy and peace shall dwell in thee, Joy and peace shall dwell in thee.

f rall. dim.

God; Joy and peace, and peace shall dwell in thee.

f

cres.

rall. dim.

Ped.

O how lovely is zion.

BLESSED ARE THE PURE IN HEART.

Slowly. (SENTENCE.) W. F. SUDDS.

Bless-ed are the pure, the pure in heart, Bless-ed are the

pure, the pure in heart, Bless-ed are the pure,

Bless-ed are the pure, the pure in heart:

For They shall see God, for they shall see God,

Bless-ed are the pure, Bless-ed are the

Bless-ed are the pure in heart, Bless-ed are the pure in heart,

pure in

Bless-ed are the pure in heart: for they shall see God, for they shall see God.

61
COME UNTO ME.
(SENTENCE.)

W. F. SUDDS.

Larghetto.

Come un-to me, Come un-to me, Come un-to me, and I will give you rest. Come un-to me, and I will give you rest. Come un-to me, Come un-to me,

Soprano Solo.
All ye that labor and are heav-y la-den and I will give you rest, I will give you rest. *Sw. Organ* D. C. al FINE.

Soft. Ped.

THE LORD IS MY SHEPHERD.

W. F. SUDDS.

Soprano: The Lord is my Shep-herd; I shall not want; The Lord is my Shep-herd; I shall not want; He mak-eth me to lie

Alto: The Lord is my Shep-herd; I shall not want;

Tenor: The Lord is my Shep-herd; I shall not want;

down in green pas - tures, And lead - eth me be - side the still wa - -

And lead - eth me be - side the still wa - -

-ters; He re - stor - eth my soul; He lead - eth me in the

-ters; He re - stor - eth my soul; He lead - eth me in the

The Lord is my Shepherd,—2.

paths of right - cousness For His

paths of right - cousness For His

name's sake.

name's sake. Yea, tho' I walk in the val - ley of the

sw.

65

I will fear no e - vil, for Thou art with me; Thy

shadow of death, I will fear no e - vil, for Thou art with me; Thy

rod and Thy staff they com - fort me. A - - men.

rod and Thy staff they com - fort me. A - - men.

THERE IS A CALM FOR THOSE WHO WEEP.

W. F. SUDDS.

1. There is a calm for those who weep, A rest for wear-y pilgrims found, They soft-ly lie, and sweetly sleep low in the ground.

2. Then travel-er in the vale of tears, To realms of ev-er-last-ing light, Tho' times dark wil-der-ness of years, pur-sue thy

Copyright, 1881, by W. F. SHAW.

dim.
ground. The storm that sweeps the wintry sky, No more disturbs their deep re -
dim.
flight, Thy soul re - newed, By grace di - vine. If God our im - age freed from
dim.
pose, Than summer evening's la - test sigh,— That shuts the rose.
clay, In heaven's e - ternal sphere shall shine a star of day.

LO, MY SHEPHERD IS DIVINE.

In part from CONCONE.

Lo, my Shep-herd is di-vine; How can I want when He is mine?

Lo, my Shep-herd is di-vine; How can I want when He is mine?

Lo, my Shep-herd is di-vine; How can I want when He is mine?

By the streams that wan-der slow, Through the meads where flow'r-ets grow, He lead-eth me, He lead-eth me, He lead-eth me, He lead-eth

By the streams that wan - der slow Through the meads where flow'r - ets grow, He lead-eth me, He lead-eth me, He lead-eth me, He lead-eth

La my Shepherd is Divine.—2.

me, And there I rest in love and peace di-vine-ly blest, And

me, And there I rest in love and peace di-vine-ly blest,

ACC. BASS ONLY.

Ped. 8vi.

there I rest in peace, ... And there I rest in

I rest in peace, I

I rest in peace, I

peace, ... And there I rest in peace, . . . di - vine -
rest, in peace,   peace, in peace,

rest   in peace, And there I   rest   in   peace, in   peace, di - vine -

GT. OP. DIA.

OP. DIA.   OFF.

ly   blest,   Di - vine - ly   blest. . . .

ly   blest,   Di - vine - ly   blest. . . .

pp   SW.

Lo, my Shepherd is Divine,—4.

THE LORD IS IN HIS HOLY TEMPLE.

Adagio.

W. F. SUDDS.

pp The Lord is in his ho - ly temple; let all the earth keep silence, keep

the earth keep si - lence.

si - lence be - fore......... him; Let all......... The

the earth keep si - lence.

the earth keep si - lence, the earth keep si - lence, *rall.*

earth......... keep si - - - lence, keep si - lence be - fore

the earth keep si - lence, the earth keep si - lence,

let all......... the earth......... keep

him, the earth keep si - ience, the earth keep si - lence,

si - - - lence keep *rall. dim.*

the earth keep si - lence, keep si - lence be - fore......... him.

PRAISE WAITETH FOR THEE.

(THANKSGIVING ANTHEM.)   W. F. SUDDS.

Soprano: Praise waiteth for Thee, Praise waiteth for Thee, Praise waiteth for Thee, O God, in Zi - on;

Organ: *With animation.* mf SW. OP. DIAP. FLUTE & STRING.

Praise waiteth for Thee, Praise waiteth for Thee, Praise waiteth for

Praise waiteth for Thee, Praise waiteth for Thee, Praise waiteth for

Add GT. OP. DIA.

Ped.

Thee, O God in Zi - on. And un - to Thee shall the

Thee, O God in Zi - on. And un - to Thee shall the

GT. OP. DIA. off.

vow be per-form-ed. O Thou that hearest prayer, Thou crownest the year with Thy

vow be per-form-ed. O Thou that hearest prayer, Thou

GT. OP. DIA.   MAN.

p ACC. BASS ONLY.

good - - ness, Thou crownest the year with thy good - ness, with thy goodness. The

Thou crownest the year with thy good - ness, with thy goodness.

crownest the year with thy good - ness, Thou crownest the year with thy goodness. The

Ped.

pastures are covered with flocks, the valleys with corn; They shout for joy, ...

_ff_

They shout for joy, they shout for joy, they shout for

pastures are covered with flocks, the valleys with corn; They shout for joy, they shout for joy, they shout for

MAN.

Add PRINCIPAL and 8 FT. REEDS.

Ped.

Solo. _mp_

. . . they al - - so sing. Praise wait - eth for Thee,

joy,

joy, they al - - so sing.

_mp_

SW. 8 FT.

Praise waiteth for Thee,—4.

Praise waiteth for Thee, Praise waiteth for Thee, O God in Zi - on;

Praise waiteth for Thee, Praise waiteth for Thee, Praise waiteth for

Praise waiteth for Thee, Praise waiteth for Thee,

ADD GT. OP. DIA. & REEDS,

Thee, Praise waiteth for Thee, waiteth for Thee, waiteth for

Praise waiteth for Thee, Praise waiteth for Thee, waiteth for

Thee, O God in Zi - on, Praise waiteth for Thee.

Thee, O God in Zi - on, Praise waiteth for Thee.

Slow. mp

Praise waiteth for Thee.— 6.

AWAKE, MY SOUL!

BEETHOVEN.

Moderato. mf

Soprano.

A - wake, my soul! A - wake, my tongue! my God de-mands the

Alto.

mf

Tenor.

A - wake, my soul! A - wake, my tongue! my God de-mands the

Bass.

Organ.

mf
GT. OF DIA.

Ped.

grate-ful song; Let all my in-most powers re-cord The wondrous mercy of the Lord.

grate-ful song; Let all my in-most powers re-cord The wondrous mercy of the Lord

His mer-cy with un - chang-ing rays, For-ev - er shines, while time de - cays; And

His mer - cy with un - chang-ing rays, For-ev - er shines, while time de - cays; And

chil - dren's chil - dren shall re - cord The truth and good - ness of the Lord.

chil - dren's chil - dren shall re - cord The truth and good - ness of the Lord.

While all His works His praise pro-claim, And men and an - gels bless His name. Oh,

While all His works His praise pro-claim, And men and an - gels bless His name. Oh,

cres.   *dim.*

let my heart, my life, my tongue, At - tend and join the bliss - ful song!

dim.

let my heart, my life, my tongue, At - tend and join the bliss - ful song!

cres.

Awake, my Soul.—3.

PROTECT US THROUGH THE COMING NIGHT.

CURSHMAN.
As a Quartette, by W. F. Sudds.

Pro - tect us through the com - ing night, O Fa - ther. O Fa - ther, might - - y, de - liv - er us from every ill, de - liv - er us from every ill, And guard our slum - -

SOPRANO.
-ber, And guard our slum - - ber. Pro - tect us through the
ALTO.
O Fa - ther
com - ing night, O Fa - ther. O Fa - ther might - -
might - - - y! O Fa - ther might - -
Ped.
cres - cen - do.
-y, de - liv - er us from every ill, de - liv - er us from every
-y, O Fa - ther, O
cres - cen do.
Ped.

dim.
rit.
mp
ill, and guard our slum - - ber, And guard our slum - ber. Pro-
dim.
Fa - - - - ther, ... - And guard our slumber.
mp
Pro-
mp
dim.
rit.
-tect us through the com - ing night. O Father, O
Father, O Father
-tect us through the com - ing night. O Father,
cres.
Ped.

cres - cen - do.

Fa - ther might - - y, de-liv-er us from every ill, de-liv-er

might - y! . O Fa - ther mighty, de-liv-er

cres - cen - do.

Fa - ther might - - y! O Fa - ther mighty, de-liv-er

cres - cen - do.

pp *rall.*

us from every ill, And guard our slum - ber, And guard our slum - -

us from every ill, And guard our slum - ber, And guard our slum - -

pp *rall.*

pp

pp *rall.*

SOFT PED.

-ber,   Protect us, Fa - ther, O Father

Protect us, Fa - ther, O Father

-ber,   Protect us, Fa - ther, O Father might-y,   Fa - - - ther

might - - - - - - - - - - y!   O Fa - ther

Pro - tect us, Fa - ther, O Fa - ther might - y!

might - y, Pro - tect us, Fa - ther, O Fa - ther might - y!

might - y,   Fa - - - ther might - y! O Fa - ther

might-y! O Father might-y, de-liv-er us from ill, And guard our

us, de-liv-er us,

might-y! O Father might-y, de-liv-er us from ill, And guard our

slum - - ber, And guard our slum - - - ber.

slum - - ber, And guard our slum - - - ber.

ROCK OF AGES.

W. F. SUDDS.

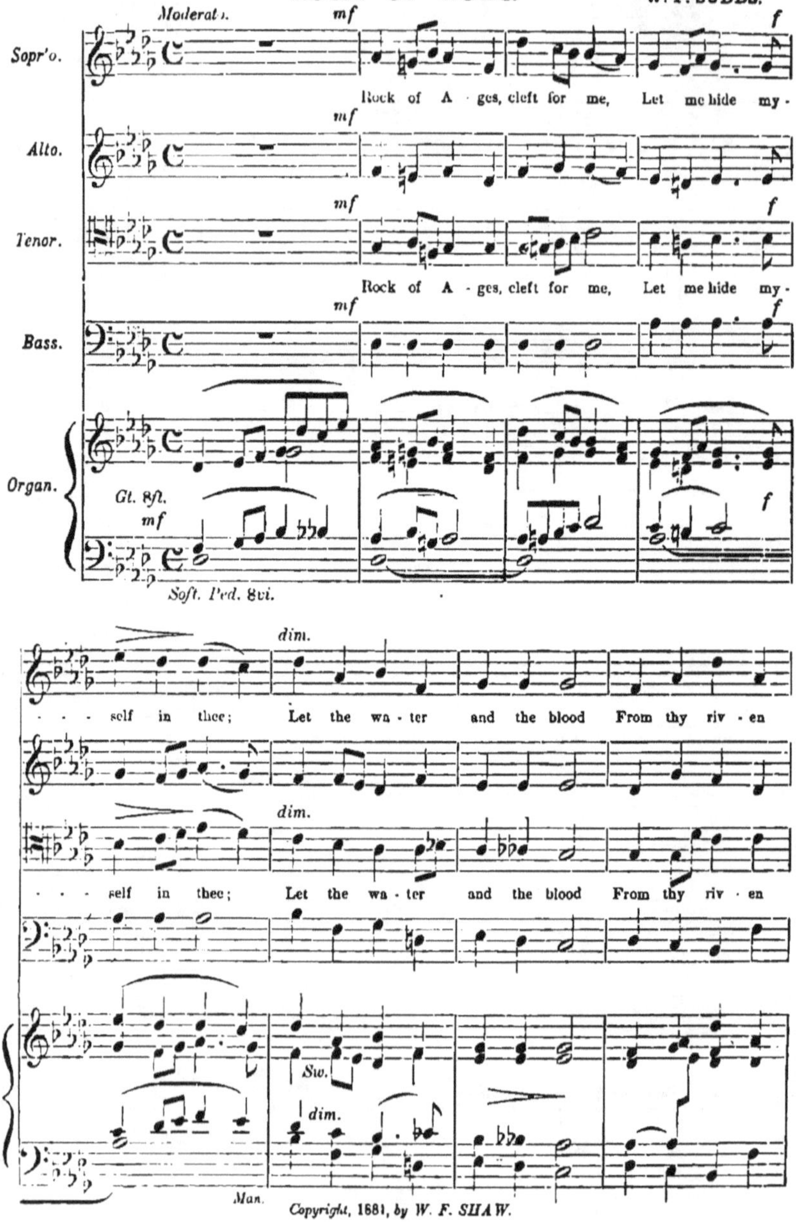

side that flow'd, Be of sin the double cure, Save from wrath, and make me pure.

side that flow'd, Be of sin the double cure, Save from wrath, and make me pure.

Gt. op. Dia.
cres.

Ped.

Soprano Solo.

Could my zeal no lan - gour know, Could my tears for ev - er flow,

Sw. Man.

rall.

All for sin could not a - tone, Thou must save and thou a - lone;

Gt.

Sw.

Ped.

Rock of Ages

In my hand no price I bring, Sim - ply to thy cross I cling.

rall.

While I draw my fleet - ing breath, When my eye - lids close in death,

While I draw my fleet - ing breath, When my eye - lids close in death,

Man.

Rock of Ages.

When I rise to worlds un-known, See thee on thy Judg-ment throne.

When I rise to worlds un-known, See thee on thy Judg-ment throne.

cres.

Op. Dia.

Ped.

Rock of a-ges cleft for me, Let me hide my-self in thee.

Rock of a-ges cleft for me, Let me hide my-self in thee.

full organ.

cres.

Rock of ages.

THE LORD IS IN HIS HOLY TEMPLE.

OTTO LOB.

The Lord is in his ho - ly tem - ple,

The Lord is in his lo - ly tem . . . . ple, in his tem . . ple,

The Lord is in his ho ly tem ple, in his tem ple, keep

mf
Keep silence, keep silence, keep silence, be - fore him. Let all the earth be
mf
mf
silence, keep silence, keep silence be - fore him. Let all the earth be
f
Piu vivo. Let all the
pp
mf
silent be - fore him. Let all the earth be si - lent be - fore him.
p a tempo.
For the Lord, the
p
silent be - fore him. Let all the earth be si - lent be - fore him. For the
earth be si - lent, Let all the earth be si - lent,
a tempo.
pp

For the Lord, the Lord is in his holy tem - ple, keep si - lence, keep

Lord,......... the Lord is in his holy tem - ple, keep silence, keep

Lord,......... the Lord is in his holy tem - ple, keep silence, keep

For the Lord is in his holy tem - - ple, keep silence,

Gt. op.   Sw.

si - lence be - fore him.   The Lord is in his ho - ly

silence be - fore him. The Lord is in his ho - ly tem - - ple, in his

silence be - fore him. The Lord is in his ho - ly tem - - ple, in his

The Lord is in his Holy Temple.

tem - ple, keep silence, keep silence, keep silence be - fore........

tem - ple, keep silence, keep silence, keep silence be - fore........

tem - ple, keep silence, keep silence, keep silence be - fore........

pp

molto ritard.

him, keep silence, be - fore him: silence, si - lence.

him, keep silence, keep si - lence be - fore him: silence, si - lence

him, keep silence, keep si - lence be - fore him: silence, si - lence.

molto ritard

p

pp ad lib

The Lord is in his Holy Temple.

NEARER, MY GOD, TO THEE.

W. F. SUDDS.

1. Near - er, my God, to Thee, Near - er to
2. There let the way appear, Steps un - to

Thee, E'en though it be a cross, That raiseth me;
heaven, All that Thou send - est me, In mer - cy given;

Still all my song shall be, Near - er, my God, to Thee, Near - er, my
An - gels to beck - on me, Near - er, my God, to Thee, Near - er, my

rit. FINE.

God, to Thee, near - er to Thee.
God, to Thee, near - er to Thee.

rit.

sw.

FINE.

SOLO.

Though like a wan - derer, Day - light all

gone, Dark - ness comes o - ver me, My rest a stone,

sw.

mf *cres* *cen* - *do.* *rit.*

Yet in my dreams I'd be Nearer, my God, to Thee, Near - er, my God, to Thee,

rit.

mf *cres* - - *cen* - - *do.* *rit.*

Yet in my dreams I'd be Nearer, my God, to Thee, Near - er, my God, to Thee,

rit.

mf

GT. OR. DIA. 'cres - - *cen* - - *do.*

Ped.

D.S.℥

Near - er to Thee.

Near - er to Thee.

D.S.℥

sw.

sw.

Nearer, my God, to Thee,—3.

SAVIOUR BREATHE AN EVENING BLESSING.

Sav - iour breathe an even - ing bless - ing, Ere re - pose our eye - lids seal. Sin and
Though the night be dark and drear - y, Dark - ness can - not hide from thee. Thou art

Saviour breathe an evening blessing.

round us........ Tho' the ar - rows past us fly,........ An - gel
take us........ And our couch be - come our tomb,...... may the

- struc - tion walk a round us past us fly...... An - gel
death this night take us to our tomb...... May the

Gt. op. Dia.

guards from thee sur - round us, We are safe if thou art nigh.
morn in heav'n a - wake us Clad in bright e - ter - nal bloom.

guards from thee sur - round us, We are safe if thou art nigh.
morn in heav'n a - wake us Clad in bright e - ter - nal bloom.

p
Sw.

Saviour breathe an evening blessing.

AS PANTS THE HART.

W. F. SUDDS.

Andante.

Organ.

p
SFT.

SOLO, for MEZZO SOPRANO, or ALTO.

SW.

1. As pants the hart for cool-ing streams, While heat-ed
2. For Thee, my God, the liv-ing God, My thirst-y

f

in the chase, ... So longs my soul, O God, for Thee, And
soul, doth pine ; . . . . . Oh, when shall I be-hold Thy face, Thou

Thy re-fresh-ing grace.
Ma-jes-ty, di-vine ?

Add 4FT. FLUTE.

As pants the Hart. — 1.

As pants the hart for cool - ing streams When
For Thee, my God, the liv - ing God, My

mp

As pants the hart for cool - ing streams When
For Thee, my God, the liv - ing God, My

mp

heat - ed in the chase, So
thirst - y soul doth pine; Oh,

So longs my soul, O
Oh, when shall I be

heat - ed in the chase, So longs my soul, O God, for Thee, So
thirst - y soul doth pine; Oh, when shall I be - hold Thy face, Oh,

As pants the Hart.—2.

God, for Thee,
hold thy face,

longs my soul, O God, for Thee, So longs my soul, O God, for
when shall I be - hold Thy face, Oh, when shall I be - hold Thy

SW. ACC. BASS ONLY.

m p cres.

Thee, So longs my soul, O God, for Thee, and Thy re - fresh-ing grace.
face, Oh, when shall I be - hold Thy face, Thou Ma - jes - ty di - vine?

mp cres.

Thee, So longs my soul, O God, for Thee, and Thy re - fresh-ing grace.
face, Oh, when shall I be - hold Thy face, Thou Ma - jes - ty di - vine?

mp

As pants the Hart. 3.

CONSIDER THE LILIES.

"TOPLIFF."
As a Quartette by W. F. SUDDS.

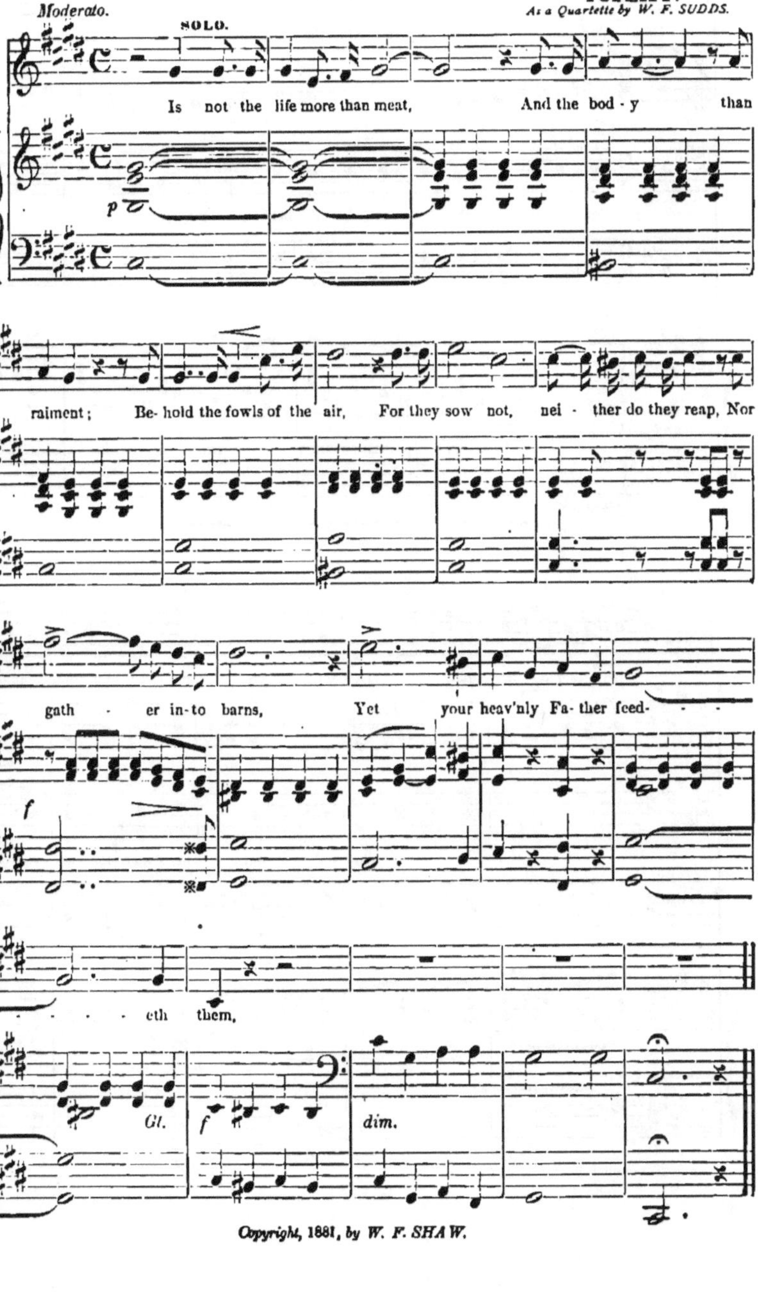

Con-sid - er the lil - ies of the field how they grow, They toil not
nei - ther do they spin, They toil not, nei - ther do they spin..........

Con-sid er the lil - ies of the field how they grow,
They toil not, nei - ther do they spin..........

Gt. stop Dia.
and Melodia.

Ped.

Consider the lilies.

And yet I say un-to you, I say un-to you that e-ven

And yet I say un-to you, I say un-to you that e-ven

cres.

cres. *f*

Solomon in all his glo ry, was not ar-ray'd like one of

f

cres.

Solomon in all his glo ry, was not ar-ray'd like one of

crs. *f*

f

Consider the lilies.

these. Con-sid-er the lil-ies how they grow, Con-sid-er the

these.

lil-ies how they grow, They toil not, they toil not nei-ther do they

They toil not, they toil not nei-ther do they

Consider the lilies.

spin, yet I say un-to you, Solomon in all his glo-ry

spin, yet I say un-to you, Solomon in all his glo-ry

Gt. op. Dia.

dim.

was not array'd, was not array'd like one of these.

was not ar-ray'd like one of these,

was not array'd, was not array'd Like one of these,

Gt. 4 ft. Flute.

dim.

Sw.

Sw.

Consider the lilies.

was not array'd,   was not array'd   like one of these.

like one of these,

And yet I say un - to you,   Solomon in all his glo - ry

Consider the lilies,

was not ar-ray'd, was not ar-ray'd, was not ar-ray'd like one of these,

was not ar-ray'd, was not ar-ray'd, was not ar-ray'd like one of these,

like one of these, like one of these.

like one of these, like one of these.

Consider the lilies.

O LORD, MOST MERCIFUL.

From "CONCONE."

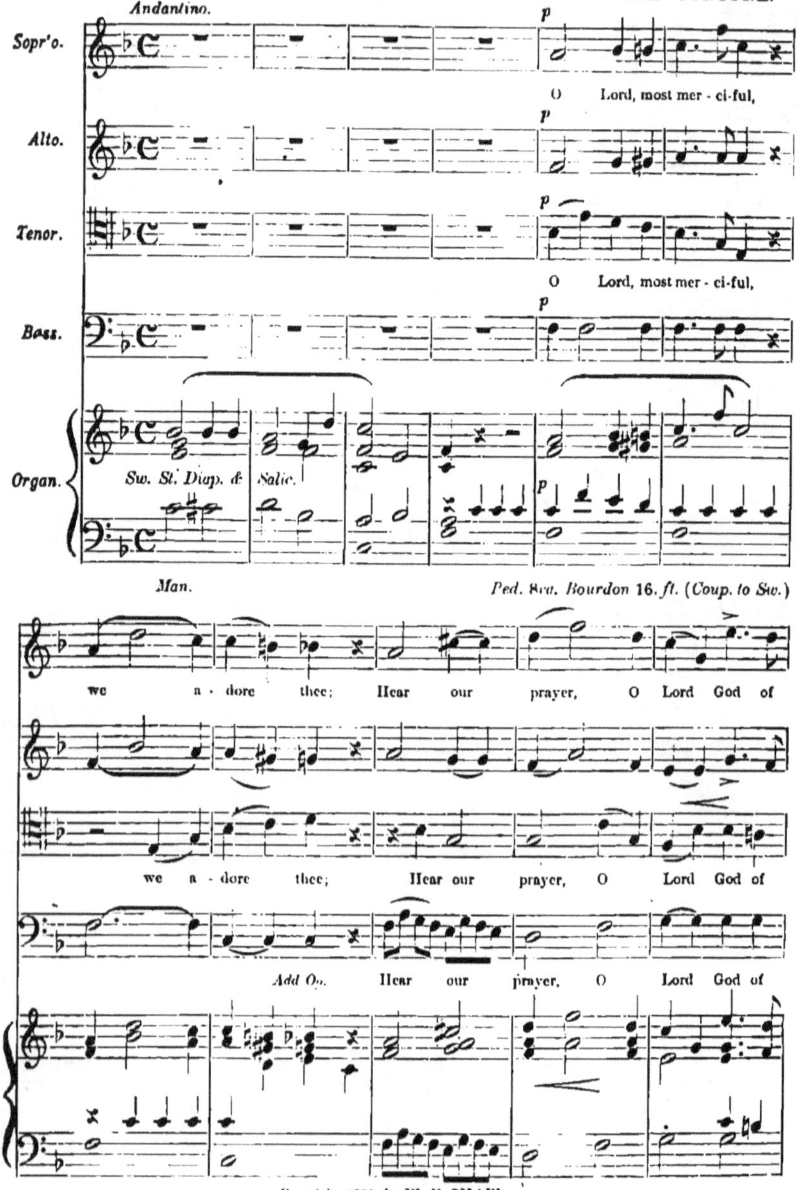

hosts. In thy great mer - cy towr'ds us draw nigh.

hosts. In thy great mer - cy, to us draw nigh.

hosts. In thy mer - cy draw thou nigh.

dolce.

Man.

Hear our prayer, O Lord most High, Hear our prayer, O..............

Hear our prayer, O Lord most High, Hear our prayer, O..............

f Gt. Diap. 8ft. Sw. p Gt. Sw.

Ped. 8vi. Op. 16ft. Ped. 8 vi. Man.

O Lord, most merciful Man.

dolce.

Lord, most High. Hide thy face............ from our sins;

Lord, most High. Hide thy face from our

Ped. Op. off.

Blot out all our in - - iq - - ui - ties; Grant us

sins; Blot out our in - iq - - - ui - ties; Grant us

O Lord, Most Merciful.

mer - cy, give us thy peace, give us thy peace for - ev - er -
Grant us mer - cy, give us thy peace, give us thy peace for ev - er -
give us thy peace, give us peace...... for ev - er -
mer - cy, give us thy peace, thy peace for ev - er -
Ped.
more. Hear, we im - plore thee; Hear, Lord, and
more. Hear we im - plore thee; Hear, Lord, and
more. Hear us and
more, Hear us and
p
Sw. Op. off.
Man.
Ped. 8vi.
Man.

save us; Hear our pe - ti - - tion, O most High; In thy great
save us, hear us, save us, O most......... High; In thy great
save us, hear us, and save us, O most High; In
Add. Op.
p
Ped.
mer - - cy tow'rds us draw nigh. Hear our prayer, O
f
p
mer - cy.................. tow'rds us.................. draw nigh. Hear our prayer, O
mer - cy, in mer - cy to us draw nigh. Hear our prayer, O
Gt. f
Sw
Ped. Op. 8vi
Man.

doux.

Lord, most High, Hear our prayer, O......... Lord, most High.

prayer, O......... Lord, most High, O Lord, most

Lord, most High. Hear our prayer, O......... Lord, most High,,

Lord, most High, Hear our prayer, O Lord, most High, O Lord, most

Gt. *f* Sw. *p*

Ped. 8vi.   Ped. Op. off. Man.

douz.   *dim.*

hear our prayer, hear our prayer, O Lord, most high.

High, hear our prayer, O Lord, most High, hear our prayer. O Lord, most High.

hear our prayer, O Lord, most High, hear our prayer, O Lord, most High.

High hear our prayer, hear our prayer, O Lord, most High.

dim.

Ped. Sw. Op. off dim.

O Lord, most Merciful.

HEAR MY PRAYER.

W. F. SUDDS.

Hear my pray'r, hear my pray'r, hear my pray'r O God, in-cline thine ear. Hear my pray'r, hear my pray'r; From my pe-ti-tion do not hide, from my pe-ti-tion do not hide; Without thee all is dark, I have no guide, without thee all is dark, I have no guide, I have no guide. Hear my pray'r, hear my pray'r. Hear my pray'r, O God in-cline thine ear. Hear my pray'r, hear my pray'r O God In-cline thine ear. A-men.

JUBILATE DEO.

In B♭.

W. F. SUDDS.

O be joyful in the Lord, O be joyful in the

O be joyful in the Lord, O be joyful in the

Organ. *Gt. Op. Diap.*

Lord, all ye lands: all ye lands:............... serve the Lord with

Lord, all ye lands: all ye lands:............... serve the Lord with glad - ness, serve the Lord with glad - ness, and come before his pres - ence with a song.

glad - ness, serve the Lord with glad - ness, and come before his pres - ence with a song.

Be ye sure that the Lord he is God; It is he that has made us and not we ourselves;

f

BASS SOLO.

m p

Jubilate Deo.

pp
We are his people,

pp

We are his peo-ple,

we are his people, and the sheep of his pasture.

rall.

rall.

f

O go your way into his gates with thanksgiving,

f

f

O go your way into his gates with thanksgiving,

f

f

Gt. op. Dia.

Jubilate Deo.

and in - to his courts with praise; Be thankful un - to him, be thankful un - to

and in - to his courts with praise; Be thankful un - to him, be thankful un - to

rall. dim.

him, be thankful unto him, and speak good of his name.

him, be thankful unto him, and speak good of his name.

rall. dim.

Jubilate Deo.

For the Lord   is gracious, for the

For the Lord   is gracious, for the

Lentando.   dim.

p   Sw.

Lord   is   gracious, His mer-cy is ev-er-lasting; and his truth en-dur-eth from gener-

Lord   is gracious; His mer-cy is ev-er-lasting; and his truth en-dur-eth from gener-

Jubilate Deo.

rall.
Allegro.
a tion to gener - a - tion.
Glo - ry, Glo ry,
a - tion to gener - a - tion
Glo - ry, Glo - ry,
rall.
Allegro.
dim.
Gt. op. Dia.
Glo - ry be to the Fa - ther, and to the Son, and to the Ho - ly
Glo - ry be to the Fa - ther, and to the Son, and to the Ho - ly

Ghost. As it was in the be-ginning, is now, and ev-er shall be world without

Ghost. As it was in the be-ginning, is now, and ev-er shall be world without

end, world without end, world with-out end. A men.

end, world without end, world with-out end. A - men.

Jubilate Deo.

EASTER ANTHEM.

W. F. SUDDS.

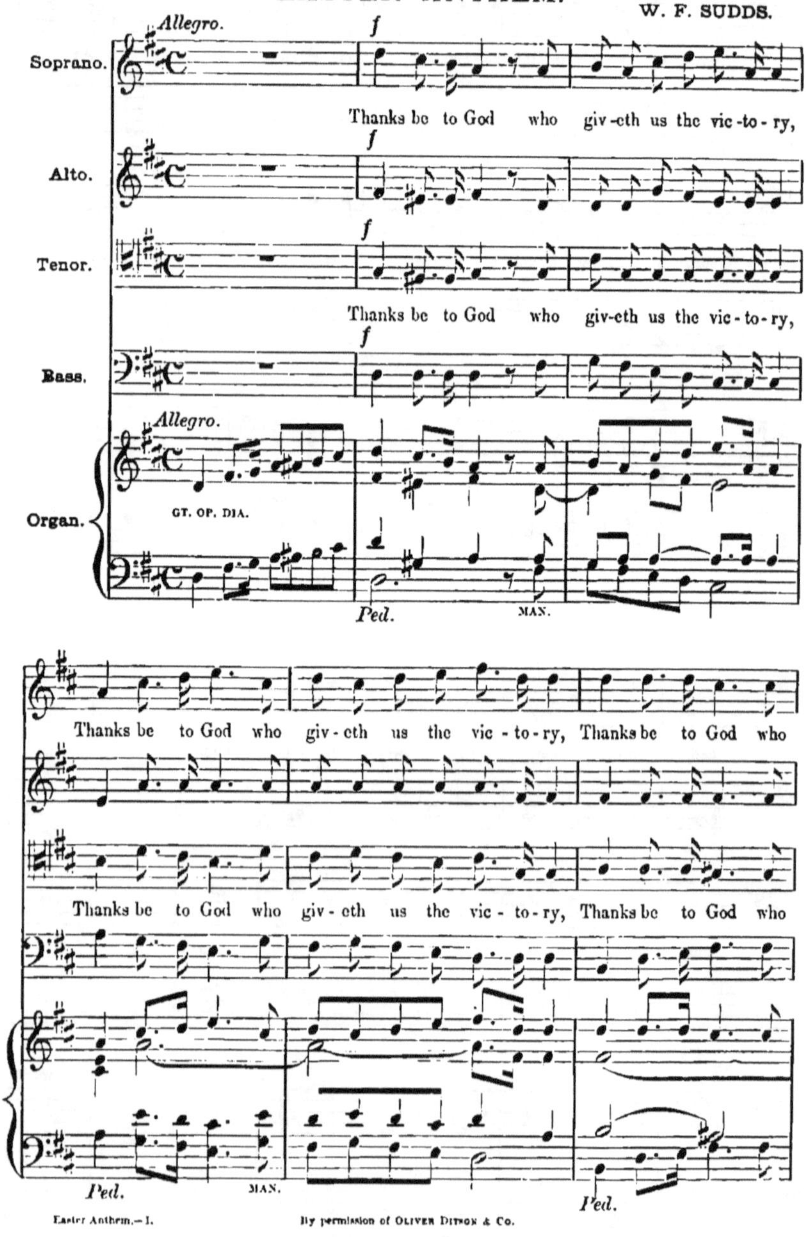

giv-eth us the vic-to-ry thro' Je-sus Christ our Lord, Thro' Je-sus Christ our

giv-eth us the vic-to-ry thro' Je-sus Christ our Lord, Thro' Je-sus Christ our

Lord. Thanks be to God who giv-eth us the vic-to-ry,

Lord. Thanks be to God who giv-eth us the vic-to-ry,

p Largo dim.

Largo dim.

SW. 8 FT.

a tempo.

a tempo.

Easter Anthem.—2.

Thanks be to God who giv-eth us the vic-to-ry, Thanks be to God who

Thanks be to God who giv-eth us the vic-to-ry, Thanks be to God who

Largo dim.

giv-eth us the vic-to-ry thro' Je-sus Christ our Lord, Thro' Je-sus Christ our

giv-eth us the vic-to-ry thro' Je-sus Christ our Lord, Thro' Je-sus Christ our

Largo dim.

Easter Anthem.—2.

He died for all, ... He died for all, . . .

mp 1st & 2nd SOPRANO. *p*

Lord. He died for all, He

p

p

Lord.

sw. *p*

died for all, He died for all that they which live might not henceforth live un-to themselves, But un - to him who died for them. He rose a - gain,

But un - to him who died for them.

SW. SFT.
pp

f a tempo.

He rose a - gain.

Thanks be to God who
f

f

Thanks be to God who
f

Tempo Imo.

GT. OP. DIA.
f

giv-eth us the vic - to-ry, Thanks be to God who giv-eth us the vic - to-ry,

giv-eth us the vic - to-ry, Thanks be to God who giv-eth us the vic - to-ry,

Thanks be to God who giv - eth us the vic - to-ry Thro'

Thanks be to God who giv - eth us the vic - to-ry Thro'

Easter Anthem,— 6.

Je - sus Christ our Lord, thro' Je - sus Christ our Lord.

Je - sus Christ our Lord, thro' Je - sus Christ our Lord.

He is ris - en, He is ris - en, Al - le - lu - ia, A - men.

He is ris - en, He is ris - en, Al - le - lu - ia, A - men.

Al - le - lu - ia, Al - le - lu - ia, Al - le - lu - ia, A -

Al - le - lu - ia, Al - le - lu - ia, Al - le - lu - ia, A -

ff

Ped.

men, A - men, A - men, A - men.

men, A - men, A - men, A - men.

ff

ff

ff

Easter Anthem.—8.

GOD BE MERCIFUL.

W. F. SUDDS.

Soprano: God be mer - ci-ful unto us, and

Tenor: God be mer - ci-ful unto us, and

bless us, And show us the light of Thy coun - tenance, And be

bless us, And show us the light of Thy coun - tenance, And be

135

mer - ci-ful,   And be mer - ci-ful un - to us,

mer - ci-ful,   And be mer - ci-ful un - to us,

That Thy way may be known up - on earth, Thy saving health a - mong all nations.

That Thy way may be known up - on earth, Thy saving health a - mong all nations.

f faster.

Let the people praise Thee, O God, Yea, let all the peo - ple praise Thee.

Let the people praise Thee, O God, Yea, let all the peo - ple praise Thee.

f spirited.

O let the na - tions re - joice, O let the na - tions re -
Let the na - tions re - joice,

O let the na - tions re - joice, O let the na - tions re -

O let the na - tions re-joice, Let the na - tions re - joice,

-joice,   O   let   the   na - tions re - joice   and be

O   let   the   na - tions re - joice,

-joice,   O   let   the   na - tions re - joice

O   let   the   na - tions re - joice, Let the na - tions re - joice   and be

glad,   For Thou shall judge the folk righteously,   And

glad,   For Thou shall judge the folk righteously,   And

gov - ern the na - tions up - on earth. Let the peo - ple praise Thee,

gov - ern the na - tions up - on earth. Let the peo - ple praise Thee,

O God, Yea, let all the peo - ple praise Thee.

O God, Yea, let all the peo - ple praise Thee.

Ped.

God be Mer - ful. 5

Then shall the earth bring forth her increase, And God, even our own God, shall give us His blessing. God shall bless us, God shall bless us, And all the ends of the earth shall fear Him.

God be Merciful.— 6.

Glo-ry, glo-ry,

Glo-ry, glo-ry,

glo-ry,   glo-ry be to the Father,   And to the   Son, and to the

glo-ry,   glo-ry be to the Father,   And to the   Son, and to the

God be Merciful.—7.

Holy Ghost, As it was in the be - gin - ning, is now, and ev - er

Ho - ly Ghost, As it was in the be - gin - ning, is now, and ev - er

cres. *cres - cen -*

slower.

shall be, World without end, A - men, World without end, A - men.

shall be, World without end, A - men, World without end, A - men.

- do. *Ped.*

God be Merciful,— 8.

IN THE HOLY LAND OF HEAVEN.

Words by WM. W. LONG.

W. F. S.*

* Poetry used by Permission.   Copyright, 1881, by W. F. SHAW.

way the murky chill; Where each day comes in new beau-ty, Calmly, quietly, and still. In the

mother find her child; There will gather shattered households, Broken in this barren wild,

never loved before; There each sinless face will brighten With sweet peace for evermore. In the

holy land of heaven We for aye shall meet and rest, Where all broken ties are gathered, We for ever shall be blest.

holy land of heaven We for aye shall meet and rest, Where all broken ties are gathered, We for ever shall be blest.

In the Holy land of Heaven.

PALM BRANCHES.

By FAURE.

Arr. for Choir use by W. F. SUDDS.

Solo or Duet.

1. O'er all the way green palms and blos-soms gay   Are strewn this day, in fes - tal
2. His word goes forth, and peo-ple by its might   Once more re-gain free-dom from
3. Sing and re-joice O blest Je - ru - sa lem.   Of all thy Sons sing the e -

pre - - - par - a - tion.
deg - - - ra - da - tion.
man - - - ci - pa - tion.

Where Je - sus comes to wipe our
Hu - man - i - ty doth give to
Through bound - less love, the Christ of

Tears a - way.
Each his right,
Beth - le - hem

E'en now the throng to wel - come
While those in dark - ness find re -
Brings faith and hope to thee for -

him pre-pare.

Join all and sing his

- - stored the light.
- - ev er more.

Join all and sing his

Join all and sing his

Palm Branches

name de-clare. Let ev - ery voice re - sound with

name de - clare.

name de - clare.

ac - cla - ma - tion. Ho - san - na,

Ho - san - na, Ho san na,

Ho - san na,

Palm Branches.

Ped.

praise be the Lord! Bless him who com-eth to bring us Sal-

praise be the Lord! Bless him who com-eth to bring us Sal-

va · · · tion.

- va - tion, to bring us Sal - va · · tion.

va · · · · · tion.

Palm Branches.

Small notes for last time.

THE DAY OF REST.

CLARIBEL.
Arr. for Choir by W. F. SUEDS.

The week is o-ver, and to-day Once more we meet to praise and pray. Once more a peace, a ho-ly calm,

The week is o-ver, and to-day once more we meet to praise and pray. Once more a peace, a ho-ly calm,

Falls on our troubled hearts like balm,   For in the week sure

Falls on our troubled hearts like balm,   For in the week sure

cres.

few could say,   No shadow fell a - cross their way;   And to some lives how doub-ly blest, The

cres.

few could say,   No shadow fell a - cross their way;   And to some lives how · doubly blest, The

Gt. cres.

The day of rest.

quiet of this day of rest. The week is over,

quiet of this day of rest. The week is over

and to-day, Once more we meet to praise and pray, Once more a peace and holy calm,

and to-day, Once more we meet to praise and pray, Once more a peace and holy calm,

Acc. Bass only.

The day of rest.

Ral - - len - - tan - - do.

Falls on our troubled hearts like balm. In this day's calm, my soul shall seek A staff to lean on

Ral - - len - - tan - - do.

alls on our troubled hearts like balm. In this day's calm, my soul shall seek A staff to lean on

cres.

through the week, And may each Sabbath prove the best, Till the e - ter - nal day of rest.

cres.

through the week, And may each Sabbath prove the best, Till the e - ter - nal day of rest.

Gt.

Sw.

The day of rest.

ABIDE WITH ME.

W. F. SUDDS.

Andan'e.

Andante.

p

Stop. Dia.

Ped.

Man.

Ped.

S.p. or Alto.

p

Tenor. A bide with me, fast falls the e - ven tide,

The dark - ness deep - ens, Lord, with me a - bide.

When oth-er help-ers fail, And comforts flee, Help of the help-less

When oth-er help-ers fail, And comforts flee, Help of the help-less

rall.

O a-bide with me.

O a-bide with me.

Abide with me.

Ped.

I need thy pres ence ev - 'ry pass-ing hour; What but thy grace can

I need thy pres - ence ev - 'ry pass-ing hour; What but thy grace can

foil the tempter's power? Who like thy - self my guide and stay can be?

Who like thy - self my guide and stay can be?

Abide with me.

Through cloud and sun-shine, Lord, a - bide with me.

Through cloud and sun-shine, Lord, a - bide with me.

I fear no foe with thee at hand to bless.

I fear no foe with thee at hand to bless.

Abide with me.

Ills have no weight. And tears no bit - ter - ness. Where is death's sting? Where

Ills have no weigth. And tears no bit - ter - ness Where is death's sting? Where

f — *Rall. dim.*

grave thy vic - to - ry? I triumph still, if thou a - bide with me.

f — *Rall. dim.*

grave thy vic - to - ry? I triumph still, if thou a - bide with me.

mf

Ra'l. dim.

Ped.

Abide with me

HOW LOVELY ARE THY DWELLING'S FAIR.

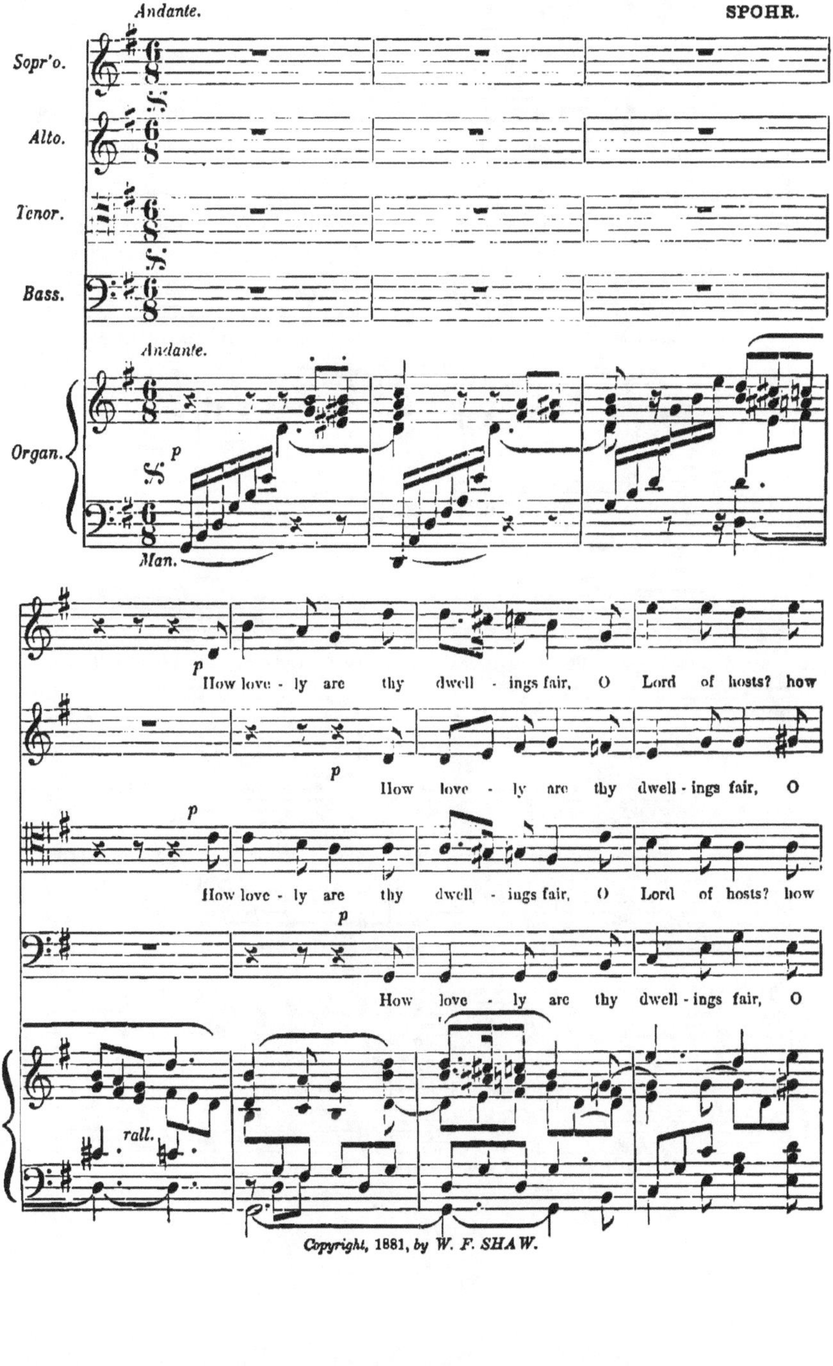

How lovely are thy dwellings fair.

dear, how dear The pleas - - ant tab - er - na - - cles are, When

Lord, how dear The pleas - - ant tab - er - a - - cles are. When

dear, how dear The pleas - - ant tab - er - na - - cles are. When

Lord, how dear The pleas - - ant tab - er - na - el are. When

Thou dost dwell so near,............. When thou dost dwell so near...........

Thou dost dwell so near, so near, When thou dost dwell so near, so near.

Thou dost dwell so near,............. When thou dost dwell so near, so near.

Thou dost dwell so near, so near, When thou dost dwell so near, so near.

How lovely are thy dwellings fair.

Soprano Solo.

My soul doth long and al - most die, thy courts, O, God, to

see. My heart and flesh a - loud do cry, O,

dim.

liv ing God, for thee, O, liv ing God, for

thee. There, e'en the spar rows freed from wrong Hat's

How lovely are thy dwellings fair.

found a house of rest. The swal - low there to lay her young Hath

built her brood - ing nest. E'en by thy al - tars,

Lord of Hosts, They find their safe a bode; And

home they fly from round the coasts to thee, my king, my God.

How lovely are thy dwellings fair.

IF MY IMMORTAL SAVIOUR LIVES?

HYMN ANTHEM.

From WEBER.

If my immor - tal Saviour lives, Then my immortal (Soprano)

If my immor - tal Saviour lives, Then my immortal (Tenor)

life is sure,...... His word a firm foun - da - tion gives; Here I may build and rest se - cure (Soprano)

life is sure,...... His word a firm foun - da - tion gives; Here I may build and rest se - cure (Tenor)

Soprano or Tenor Solo.

Here let my faith un - sha - ken dwell, For - ev - er sure the prom - ise stands.

Sw.

rall.

Not all the pow'rs of earth or hell, Can e'er dis - solve the sa - cred bands.

rall.

If my Immortal Saviour lives?

Here O my soul, thy trust repose, If Jesus is for - ev - er mine?

Here O my soul, thy trust repose, If Je - sus is for ev - er mine?

Not death itself, that last of foes Shall break a un - - ion so di - vine.

Not death itself, that last of foes Shall break a un - - ion so di - vine.

If my Immortal Saviour lives?

SUN OF MY SOUL.

W. F. SUDDS.

Sun of my soul, Thou Sa- viour dear, It is not night if thou be near;

Oh, may no earth - born cloud a - rise To hide, to

hide, to hide thee from thy ser - vant's eyes.

*May be sung by Mezzo Soprano, Alto or Bass.   *Copyright, 1881, by W. F. SHAW.*

pp
When the soft dews of kind - ly sleep My weary eye - lids gent - ly steep,
pp
gent - ly, gent - ly
When the soft dews of kind - ly sleep My weary eye - lids gent - ly steep,
gent - ly, gent - ly
Be my last thought how sweet.............................. to rest For - ev - er
steep,........................ How sweet to rest For ev - er on For
Be my last thought how sweet to rest For ev - er on, For
steep,........................ how sweet........................... to rest..................... For

on,...................... For ev - er on my Sa - viour's breast.

ev - - er on,

ev - - er on, For ev - er on my Sa - viour's breast.

ev - - - - er.

p

A - bide with me from morn till eve, For without thee I can - not live·

Abide with me from morn till eve, For with - out thee I

Sun of my Soul.

A - bide with me when night is nigh, For with - out thee, with - out thee, For
can - not live; A - bide with me when night is nigh, For with - out thee, For
with - out thee I dare not die. Come near and bless us when we wake.
with - out thee I dare not die. Come near and bless us when we wake.

Ere through the world our way we take, Till in the o - cean of

way, our way we take,............ Till in the o - cean

Ere through the world our way we take, Till in the o - cean of thy love we

way, our way we take............ Till in............ the

love we lose, our lose We lose our-selves in heaven a-bove.

of thy love We lose our-selves,

lose our-selves in heav'n a - bove, We lose ourselves in heav'n a-bove.

o - - - cean of our love,

Sun of my soul.

GOD OF MERCY.

From "COSTA."

Solo, Alto or Bass.

mf

Andante.

mp

Gt. stop Diap.

God of mer-cy, God of grace, O re-store thy sup-pliant race, Hear our sad re-pent-ant songs, Thou to whom all praise be-longs. Thou to whom all praise be-longs.

God, of mer - cy, God of grace, O re - store thy sup - pliant race;

God of mer - cy, God of grace, O re - store thy sup - pliant race.

O re - store thy suppliant

Hear, O hear us, Hear our

Hear, O hear us.

Hear; us, Hear our

Hear, O hear

pp Sw. *Gt. mf*

God of mercy.

dim.

sad   re - pent - ant songs,   Hear   our sad   re - pent - ant

Hear, O   Hear,   our songs.

sad   re - pent - ant songs,   Hear,   O Hear,   Hear,   O

dim.

songs,   Thou   to   whom   all   praise be - longs.

Hear,   O   hear   us,   hear   our   songs. Hear, O

hear,   thou   to   whom   all   praise   be - longs.

God of mercy.

Thou to whom all praise, all

Hear our sad re - pent - ant songs praise,

Hear our sad re - pent - ant songs, Thou to whom all

praise be longs, Hear, O hear our sad re - pent - ant songs.

Hear our songs, O Hear our sad re - pent - ant songs,

God of mercy.

GLORY TO GOD ON HIGH.

Tenor or Soprano.

MOZART.

Andante.

mf
Glo - ry to God on high,

Let heav'n and earth re - ply, Glo - ry to God on high, praise ye his

name; Join ye ransomed race, prais - - ing his name,

our Lord and God to bless, praising his name, our Lord and

God to bless, prais-ing his name.

Glory to God on high, let heav'n and earth reply, Glo-ry to God on high; praise ye his name.

Glory to God on high, let heav'n and earth reply, Glo-ry to God on high; praise ye his name.

Gt. op. Dia.

Glory to God on high.

Sop. Solo.

Hail him, hail him, gra - cious King, And thro' all

Gt.
Sw.

a - - ges let us sing, And thro' all a - - ges

let us sing. Through all a - ges, let us sing.

Through all a - ges, let us sing.

Glory to God on high.

Praise him, praise him, heaven - ly King, praise, O praise him, heaven - ly King. A - - - men. A - - - men.

Praise him, praise him, heaven - ly King, praise, O praise him, heaven - ly King. A - - - men. A - - - men.

Glory to God on high.

FATHER I KNOW THY WAYS ARE JUST.

W. F. SUDDS.

Alto or Mezzo Soprano Solo.

mp
Fa-ther I know thy ways are just, Tho' all to me un - known,.........
to me un-known,
mp
Fa-ther I know thy ways are just, Tho' all to me un - known,.........
to me unknown,
Add 4ft Flute.
dim.
O grant me grace thy love to trust, And cry thy will be done.
dim. thy will be done.
O grant me grace thy love to trust, And cry thy will, thy will be done.
be done..................
dim.
mf
Father I know thy ways are just.

If thou should'st hedge with thorns my path, And wealth and friends be gone, Still with a live - ly faith I'll cry, Thy will, O God, be done, Thy will, O God, be done.

Al - though thy steps I can - not trace, Thy Sov - ereign right I

Al - though thy steps I can - not trace, Thy Sov - ereign right I

Father I know thy ways are just.

own　And so in - struc - ted by thy grace, I'll cry thy will be

own　And so in - struc - ted by thy grace, I'll cry thy will be

Gt. op. Dia.

f

rall. dim.

done,　Thy will, O God, be done.....................

done, thy will,　done, Thy will be done.

rall. dim.

done, thy will, Thy will, O God, be done, thy will be done.

done,...................　done.....................

rall. dim.

Ped.

Father I know thy ways are just.

O PARADISE.

BARNBY.

Moderato.

Sopr'o.
1. O Par - a - dise, O Par - a - dise, Who doth not crave for
2. O Par - a - dise, O Par - a - dise, The world is grow-ing

Alto.
3. O Par - a - dise, O Par - a - dise, Where fore doth death de-

Tenor.
4. O Par - a - dise, O Par - a - dise, 'Tis wea - ry wait - ing

Bass.

Organ. *mp*

rest, Who would not seek that hap - py land, Where they that loved are
old, Who would not be at rest and free, Where love is nev - er

lay, Bright death that is the wel - come dawn, Of our e - ter - nal

here, I long to be where Je - sus is, To feel to see him

blest. Where loy - al hearts and true stand ev - er in the
cold. Where loy - - - al hearts and true stand ev - er in the

day. Where loy - al hearts and true stand ev - er in the

near. Where loy - - al hearts and true stand ev - er in the

light, All rapt - ure thro', and thro', in God's most ho - - - ly sight.

light, All rapt - ure thro', and thro', in God's most ho - ly sight.

O Paradise.

AS THE HART PANTS.

MENDELSSOHN.

As the Hart pants af-ter the

As the Hart pants after the water-brooks,

wa - ter-brooks, so panteth my soul for Thee, O God, as the Hart pants af - ter the

As the Hart pants

As the

as the Hart pants after the wa - ter - brooks so panteth my soul for Thee, O God,

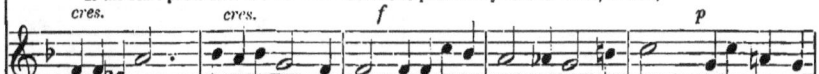

water-brooks, pants after the wa - ter-brooks, so panteth my soul for Thee, O God, so panteth my

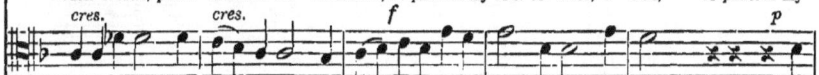

after the wa - ter-brooks, the wa - ter-brooks, so panteth my soul for Thee, O God, for

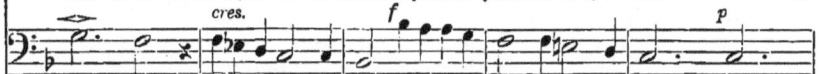

Hart pants after the wa - ter-brooks, so panteth my soul for Thee, O God, for

scen - do.

As the Hart pants.

so panteth my soul for Thee, O God, for Thee, as the Hart

soul for Thee, O God, my soul for Thee, O God, as the Hart

panteth my soul for Thee, so pant-eth my soul for Thee, O God, as the

Thee, O God, so panteth my soul for Thee, O God, as the

cres - cen do.

pants after the wa - ter-brooks, so panteth my soul for Thee, O God,

after the wa - ter-brooks, so panteth my soul for Thee, so

Hart after the wa - ter-brooks, so panteth my soul for Thee, O God, so

Hart after the wa ter-brooks, so panteth my soul for Thee, O God,

As the Hart pants.

my soul .... for thee, O God,

pant - eth my soul for thee, O God, thee, O God,

pant - eth my soul, so pants my soul for thee, O God,

thee, O God, so pants my soul for thee, O God,

sf

p

As the Hart

As the Hart

As the Hart pants.

As the Hart pants.

for Thee, O God, ... O God, Thee, O God, for Thee, O

for Thee, O God, ... O God, Thee, ... for Thee, O

God, Thee, O God, ... O God, ... for Thee, O God, ...

.... for Thee, O God, O God, ... so panteth my soul .... for

God, as the Hart pants after the water-brooks, so panteth my soul for Thee, O God, ...

God, as the Hart pants after the water-brooks, so panteth my soul for Thee, O God, ...

as the Hart pants after the water-brooks, so panteth my soul for Thee, O God, ...

Thee, as the Hart pants after the water brooks, so panteth my soul for Thee, O God, ...

As the Hart pants.

TEACH ME, O LORD.

(SENTENCE.)

W. F. SUDDS.

Teach me, O Lord, Teach me, O Lord, . . .
Teach me, O Lord, . . . Teach me, O
Teach me, O Lord, . . . Teach me, O
Teach me, O Lord, Teach me, O

. . Teach me, O Lord, the way of thy statutes, And I will keep it, will keep it un-

Lord,

Lord, Teach me, O Lord, the way of thy statutes, And I will keep it, will keep it un-

Copyright, 1881, by W. F. Shaw.

-to the end. Teach me, teach me, teach me, O Lord, Teach me,

-to the end. Teach me,

GT. DIA. off. mp

teach me, teach me, O Lord, the way of Thy statutes, And I will keep it un - to the end.

teach me, teach me, O Lord, the way of Thy statutes, And I will keep it un - to the end.

p sw.

Teach me, O Lord,—1.

f
And I will glo-ri-fy Thy name, And I will glo-ri-fy Thy name, Thy
And I will glo-ri-fy Thy name, And I will glo-ri-fy Thy
GT. 8 FT. DIA.
1
2
p
name for-ev - er-more. ev - er-more. A - - men.
name for-ev - er-more. ev - er-more. A - - men.
SW.
Ped.